THE BIOLOGY OF CONSCIOUSNESS

AND OTHER POEMS

BY

THOMAS J. ERICKSON

PEBBLEBROOK
PRESS

Published by Pebblebrook Press
an imprint of Stoneboat
PO Box 1254
Sheboygan, WI 53082-1254
Editors: Rob Pockat, Signe Jorgenson, Lisa Vihos, Jim Giese
www.stoneboatwi.com/pebblebrook-press.html

The Biology of Consciousness and Other Poems ©2016 Thomas J. Erickson
Library of Congress Catalog Card Number: 2016904466
ISBN: 978-0692669716

All rights reserved. No part of this publication may be reproduced or transmitted in any form or by any means, electronic or mechanical, including photocopy, recording, or any information storage and retrieval system, without the prior written permission of the publisher.

Cover art: *Cathedral* by Jeffrey W. Jenson ©2016

Printed in the United States

Acknowledgments

I thank the editors of the following publications, where the poems below first appeared:

About Place Journal: "The Tree"

City Lights: "The Crickets Go Silent"

FreeFall: "Sweating the Bottle"

Free Verse: "The Lost Boy"

Hartford Avenue Poets anthology *Masquerades and Misdemeanors* (Pebblebrook Press, 2013): "Light," "Word," "I Had a Dream"

The Labletter: "My Nausicaä," "Refugia"

Linden Avenue Literary Journal: "Agnosto 2013"

The Los Angeles Review: "For a Crow" (appears in this collection as "Ghazal for a Crow")

Mad Poets Review: "Berlin Sky"

Mobius: The Journal of Social Change: "The Quiddity of a Thing"

Origins: "The Worms in Ricky's Pants"

Poetry Depth Quarterly: "The Summer Hour"

Portage Magazine: "A History of the World"

SLANT: "It Began with Ice"

SNReview: "The Octopus" (appears in this collection as "Octopus")

The Line Up: Poems on Crime: "The Breathing Lesson"

Verse Wisconsin: "Momentum"

Verse Wisconsin Online: "New Year's Eve, Milwaukee, 2011"

Wisconsin Fellowship of Poets 2015 Calendar: "Trout Fishing"

Word Riot: "Speaking in Tongues," "The Gyre"

The following poems appear in the chapbook *The Lawyer Who Died in the Courthouse Bathroom* (Parallel Press, 2013): "Court Appearances," "Home Visit," "I Had a Dream," "The Floating Man," "Two Crows, the Hawk, and a Snow Shovel"

Table of Contents

Prologue   9

The Lost Boy   11
Picking Up Garbage on Tuesday Morning in the Summer   12
The Worms in Ricky's Pants   14
Savior   15
Trout Fishing   16
Two Crows, the Hawk, and a Snow Shovel   17
Another Poem About Writer's Block   18
Godzilla vs. Mothra   19
My Bactrian Funeral   20
The Quiddity of a Thing   21
A History of the World   22
Light   23
Bedbug   24
Octopus   25
Blind Date   26
The Biology of Consciousness   27

The Crickets Go Silent	29
Last Call	30
New Year's Eve, Milwaukee, 2011	32
Sweating the Bottle	33
Basketball at 51	34
Phone	35
The Chinese Proverb	36
Word	37
Speaking in Tongues	38
Reasonable Doubt	39
Burden of Proof	40
The Breathing Lesson	41
St. Augustine	42
Court Appearances	43
Home Visit	44
The Floating Man	45
Between Witnesses	46
Ghazal for a Crow	47

III

The Summer Hour	49
Berlin Sky	50
Memorial	51
Agnosto 2013	52
The Tree	53
Milwaukee	54
I Had a Dream	58
My Nausicaä	59
February 14, 2015	60
Refugia	61
Momentum	62
The Flood	63
The Gyre	64
It Began with Ice	65
Become Stone	66
The River	67
About the Author	69

Prologue

Holes in paper open and take me fathoms from anywhere.
　　　　　　　　　　　　　　　—Samuel Beckett

So much depends on a white sheet of paper,
the small boats of letters
floating on a rectangular ocean,
a sea of time

You swim to the shoals,
dive to the wreck, drift back to your youth

And after a beginning, you come to the reef
that we must all go over

and you are no longer at your desk

You've made it to the lonely shore
where all that is
is the trail of words,
the oceanic swell of your heartbeat

I

The Lost Boy

He was always in front of me
like a shadow in the late afternoon.

On this day, he runs ahead of the other
kids on the path to the lake. Just
takes off and doesn't look back.

The fork has ended at a shallow stream.
I push through the tag alders and
ford the river. *Ford* is a word I taught
him last summer, along with *eloquent,
infallible, gerund,* and a *surfeit* of others.

I call his name over and over.
With each silent reply, it is harder for me
to breathe. I run as fast as I can.
even falling takes so long—

As I sit in the dead leaves and pine
needles, daubing my cuts and looking
at my blisters, I get up and start walking.
The world has never looked so wide.

Picking Up Garbage
on Tuesday Morning in the Summer

Holding on to
the side of
the truck we
zoom
to the next
corner.
My hair
flops in the breeze;
the sweat dries
on my forehead.
I leap
to the curb
tossing
two wet plastic
bags of grass
into
the bin. A can of
corncobs
gnawed bones
watermelon
and beans is
sprinkled with
white maggots.

Another
can is
stacked with *Time*
magazines
books and
newspapers. I
sort through the
books and
salvage two. The
final can contains
charcoal ashes.
As I pour
the ash,
the dust showers
over me.
Shirtless,
sweaty, I am
covered by gray soot.
Today,
I do not
pick up garbage,
I collect it.

The Worms in Ricky's Pants

I would meet my third-grade teacher,
Miss Plotz, and some of my classmates
in a wooded ravine at seven o'clock
on Wednesday mornings to bird watch.
Miss Plotz was tall, slender, and stern—
an egret of a woman.
She loved birds so I loved birds.

Earlier, in the quiet of my house,
as my father and sisters slept,
my mother and I would squabble
over what to wear on my expedition:
boots or tennis shoes, a sweatshirt or coat.

My mother, tall but not so stern,
would send me off with a turkey
and margarine sandwich
pressed into wax paper
with aerodynamic precision.

In school, a girl told Miss Plotz
that Ricky had a worm in his desk.
Miss Plotz asked me to take Ricky
outside. We walked to the playground
and I watched him pull the
earthworms out of his pockets and drop
them to the ground.

Later that day, the kids teased
Ricky during recess and some
of them beat him up.

A week later, Ricky showed up
to bird watch. We walked through the woods—
an old maid schoolteacher,
four little girls,
Ricky, and me.

And we all looked up
into the trees.

Savior

Once when I was a little kid, and I swear this is really true,
I prayed that I would get one of my migraines.
And I did. And the black jackal came like he always did,
after the witching hour but before the birds sang,
and in the darkest dark I knew I had to crawl as fast
as I could to the bathroom to vomit whatever was good
out of me, and for a few seconds I could rest my head
on the white cool porcelain while my mom got the cot ready.
And I would lie there in the bathroom—
one movement of my head or sliver of light would
make the jackal mad and he would take his poker
and stab me right above my right eye and then the bile
would rise and he'd get what was left.

But the next day or maybe the day after, I could open
my eyes to the day and keep down some 7UP
and play Scrabble with Mom. And he was gone.
Gone.

Trout Fishing

My grandmother was a bear
of a woman. I put my arms around
her neck and she carried me over
the deep holes of the trout stream.
When our worms ran out, I used
my numb fingers to turn over
the rocks and snag salamanders—
a tiny bubble of blood where she hooked
them through their soft heads. We put
the line in low, sinkers carrying
the bait deep into the dark, cold water.
And the trout went wild.

Two Crows, the Hawk, and a Snow Shovel

Above the scrape of the shovel, I hear
two crows. I can't bring myself to buy
a snow blower even though I live
on a corner lot. Truth be told, I like
to shovel these miles of concrete.
"Offer it up," my mother would have said.

When I was a server I fainted on the altar—
overcome either by the smell of incense or my head
cold. I couldn't light the waxy, wicked candles
and Father O'Connor said "Erickson, light
those damn candles" under his breath and then I fell.

My confirmation name was Mathias
because I liked the character in *The Omega Man*
who wanted to kill Charlton Heston.
He was the last man on Earth.
When the archbishop said my name
I could feel his spittle on my forehead.

I pulled the rope that rang the bells
before mass, the heels of my black shoes
flush on the knot. Up I went.
There was a pause at the top
and it felt like I was never coming down.

The crows are wedging a hawk through
the noon sky, away from the direction of their lives,
or whatever secret they keep in the trees.

Another Poem About Writer's Block

I can't write about the time
in Little League when I tripped
over third base trying to catch
a pop-up, falling face first
in front of the Plymouth Panthers'
bench. Everyone laughed at me.
Even the umpire, who was my dad.

And I can't write about walking across
the Kingston Plains with my brother
to get way upriver where
no one fished for brook trout that summer,
stumbling upon an old bear stand
with desiccated cattle parts spiked to
splintered 2x4s rising toward
the Upper Peninsula sky
like some unlit pagan pyre.

And I can't write about being
in that very trout stream when I was
fourteen and stepping into a sinkhole
and I was stuck, really stuck, until
my dad, who was trailing me and
scavenging all the trout I missed,
dug me out—handful by handful
of sand and water and loam. Otherwise,
I'd still be in that river—my bag of bones
floating to and fro in the summer and
frozen still in the winter.

And I can't write about getting
the phone call today from my dad
who wanted to talk about the NCAA
tournament and how two 15s beat two 2s
within three hours. Now that's poetry.

Godzilla vs. Mothra

I watch my son watch Godzilla fight Mothra,
his small hands moving mechanically
from popcorn bowl to mouth. His jaw drops
in awe as Godzilla shoots red laser beams
at Mothra, the scaly-winged reptilian nightmare of Japan.

What of this Godzilla who rose from the ashes
of Hiroshima to terrorize the world and kill
the curious yet obtuse King Kong
but then, inexplicably, saved the world
from the Smog Monster? Perhaps Godzilla
is a moral relativist—he hates humans
but loves humanity. He has no problem eating
one of us but will risk his life to protect
us from our pollution-spawned predator.

My son pretends that he is Godzilla.
He sees only the monster's nobility, and
Godzilla's flaws pale by the light
of his honor. My son sees the better
part of himself, and it is true.

As the bloodied Mothra is swallowed
into the China Sea, a young boy utters solemnly,
"Thanks a million, Godzilla!" The boy
speaks for all of Japan. Indeed,
speaks for my son,
and as well, for me.

My Bactrian Funeral

The Bactrians lived in what is now northern Afghanistan circa 100 CE. When a Bactrian king died, he was buried in a large trench with his cook, his most trusted manservant, his groom, and one of his concubines, all of whom were strangled to death.

What if the great trick of it all is
that whatever you believe will happen
after you die *does* happen?
Those who believe in heaven and lead
a good life truly do go to the pearly gates.
Those who believe in hell and lead a bad
life go to the furnace with the licking
flames amidst a perpetual smell of burnt
toast. Those who believe there is nothing
are rewarded with listening to
"Dust in the Wind," thinking I told you so,
and then evaporating into the ether.
And if you blow yourself up to get 27 virgins,
good for you.

Who would accompany me to eternity?
The easy ones would be my barber Gene,
Ted the bartender, the guy who changes my oil,
Dr. Rosenberg who treats my psoriasis.
But who else? I'm thinking about everyone
who has been swallowed up by time
and distance. Minnie the Filipino girl who went with me to
the Weather Report concert in London
in 1980; Loras Feeney, the Pearl Harbor survivor
who taught me how to play cribbage at the bar;
Mikey, who I jumped off the train trestle with
just in time when we were ten.
Where the hell are you guys, so many of you
bubbling up here at the end—
a parade of supporting actors in this comedy?

And to you, my dear, I will say "Farewell,
my concubine," to make you laugh. Don't worry,
though, you are not going in the trench.
Who would take care of the dog?

The Quiddity of a Thing

In this room, we pretended
this bed was a boat. We were
in the middle of a storm, and I
rocked the mattress, almost
tossing you off, or I was a bridge
and you would crawl over me
above the dangers of Snake River.

In this room, there is a large bin
of Legos and building blocks.
We constructed our manors
and castles before tumbling them down.

In this room, the glow-in-the-dark
stars are falling from the ceiling and
there is a bed where we lay
on our backs and gazed
at the universe above our heads.

A History of the World

I.

There are so many objects in it—
lawn chairs, mirrors, maps, rulers.
History is made when objects collide.

II.

The Friday nights in summer
when I drove through the towering cornfields
of central Illinois to get to your farmhouse
in time to have a beer on the porch.
We would lie in bed with the window fan
blowing on us. The humming of the insects
like a hypnotist's command to float away.

III.

This room, where I stood by the crib,
lifted the blanket, and let the barely-
perceptible rise of tiny ribs meet
my touch. Now, I can erase the faded
pencil marks on the door jamb
with a touch of my finger.

IV.

The night I held your feet when
they were so cold they felt wet.
I took your shoes and socks off
right in the bar.

It was a simple thing, just a gesture.
It was not supposed to become
a part of the lacunae between loves.

It was not supposed to become a memory.

Light

Your check engine light is on
again. Just ignore it, it will go
away. The pilot light is dying
and we are freezing.

The soft light on your face
in the breaking dawn reminds me
of the light in your eyes years ago.

When I'm in an airplane at night
I like to see the lights next
to the dark outline of a river—
a bar, a bait shop, a house.

Bedbug

Our love is so thigmotactic—
we like rough surfaces
and we avoid the light.

Your bites don't hurt
but I have to leave
my shirt on when
I'm at the beach.

I forget you are around
during the day, but at night
I start to itch, and by daybreak
I'm exhausted.

I know you're never going
away. I'd wash these sheets,
but why take the chance.

Octopus

Thaw a three-pound octopus for a few hours in a couple of changes of cold water. Cut off the skinny tips of the tentacles (it's best to use scissors) and then cut the eight tentacles from the head. Discard the head. It will look like the head of a human, however small and squishy.

Put the octopus in a large pot of boiling water, cover and simmer for at least an hour, until it is tender. Cut potatoes into half-inch slices and cook with the octopus for another half an hour.

Drain. Put the potatoes on plates and top them with the octopus. Drizzle liberally with Spanish paprika, olive oil and sea salt.

Set the table, the one you inherited from your parents. Gather a bouquet of peonies from the garden as a centerpiece. Pour the wine. Imagine the tentacles reaching out to the four directions, the four winds.

Blind Date

She is wearing a sleeveless top
that shows off her fit arms.
Her face is pretty but her left eye
wanders and I find myself watching
it at the expense of her other eye
and the rest of her face.

She goes to church and sings
in the choir. I feel like quoting
Frost: *There is no future life...*
I see all salvation
limited to here and now.
But I can't bring myself to be that cold.

Sometimes I think I have a heart
like a Roman midden—
a mound of refuse
burying a human settlement.

I try to refuse to watch
her left eye wander but by now
I am unarmed. I need a rest.

When she returns from the restroom,
the end is in sight.

I end up where I was before.
A little further away,
more or less.

The Biology of Consciousness

Here are the words. Here are the poems
less the nuance, any implied dandyism
evaporating behind the ink of your now
absent self.

Here are the sculptures. Take away
the form and the space, the rack and the wood.
It is only gravity and glue.

The stone and the language,
indeed the very idea of sculpture and poetry,
will pass away in time.

*

I have not been in this house
before but to enter is to remember

how the capillaries connect
the dream from room to room

how the quotidian tasks line the walls

how the kitchen knife cuts
through the carapace

how the amanuensis takes down the words
and writes them on the mirrors.

The Crickets Go Silent

More and more male crickets on the island
of Oahu are born without the ability to chirp.
It seems the crickets have adapted in order
to be less vulnerable to a parasitic fly
attracted to their chirping. The male
crickets that don't chirp cannot attract females as easily
as those that do, so the quiet ones have started
staying close to the singing males, the ones
who are about to succumb.

It is November, 1980, and the newsstands read
Reagan *El Presidente!* Me and Sam
and Steve and Dave are walking around
the Prado in Madrid with Nancy and Nancy,
two tall blondes who are our American classmates
and way out of our league. Somewhere near
Titian's *The Fall of Man*, Carlos approaches.
He is impeccably dressed and looks
like a young Ricardo Montalbán. He engages
the Nancys and offers to guide them through
the exhibits while we tag along. We make
plans to meet up that night so Carlos can
show us the night life. We wait for the Nancys
past midnight at a flamenco bar but they don't
come. Carlos is peeved; we are used to it.

He's a good guy, though, and after more
sangria he takes us on the town. In the discos
and pubs, we stick by Carlos, trying to pick up
his rejects, and me and Sam and Steve and Dave
walk back to our hotel in the early morning
and we are heartened to know, in our sugary tipsiness,
just how close we were to getting laid in Madrid.

Last Call

Of course, no one believes we hit forty bars in one night.
But yes, children, we did, in an endless summer night
in the timeless burg known as Sheboygan, Wisconsin,
the Year of Our Lord Ronald Reagan, 1981.

It was me and Greg and Dave and Al and Scott and
we started at six o'clock on a Friday night.
Dave was driving his dad's car.

These were the last of the halcyon days of Sheboygan
bars when there was still a bar on every corner and
the drinking age was a blessed 18 and if you took
the "U"—Indiana to Eighth Street to Michigan—
there was a domino row of taverns, tippling one
into the other with a beautiful hazy momentum.

The rules were one tap beer (Pabst or Kingsbury or Miller)
(usually eight to twelve ounces) (if you do the math,
by the end of the night, that's at least 400 ounces
of beer—the equivalent of 33 bottles of beer for each of us)
(which isn't really all that much in eight hours for a kid
who was 20 years old in Sheboygan County where
and when beer ruled the world) (the taps were anywhere
from 25 cents to 40 cents so we spent about $15 each
which wasn't too bad because I was making $3.35 an hour
picking up garbage) (the cheapest was 15 cents
at the 1136 Tap) and various other rules depending on
our whims per bar: slam; no one talks; pinky extended;
salt your beer; French, anyone?

Andy's Bar, Ziggy's, Head East, The 1136 Tap,
Four of a Kind, Pool Tap, The Blue Room, The Tipo,
The 99 Club, Harbor Lights, the K and R Saloon, Cecil's
Palace, Mr. Glen's, Dick Suscha's Coho Bar, Who's Inn,
and so many more sunk these days by drunk driving laws
and/or the allure of drinking at home watching Netflix
or naughty things on the Internet.

Later, we bragged of our exploits. If you knew us back
then you would have believed it because it was well
established that Al and I had drunk a quarter-barrel
by ourselves and the other guys were no weak-tits either.

And why not brag? We were all heroes
that moment at bar time when
we were staggered and weak-kneed
and somehow still standing.

Before the marriages
and the kids
and the jobs.

Before we pressed on.

New Year's Eve, Milwaukee, 2011

I only go out to get a fresh appetite
for being alone; that was Byron.
I only go out to get the bag
on; that was me.

Down to the dingy bar I go. Say goodbye
Catullus to the shores of Asia Minor. Say
goodbye Tom to the curbs of Whitefish Bay.

My favorite color is Glenlivet brown and tonight
I'm going to prove it. It's only twelve years old
but I'm going to make it my bitch.

I hope I see Jimmy, but he's probably making
popcorn for the crowd at the Globetrotter game.
I'd like to play cribbage with Mike, but he's dead.
At least Ed the heroin-addict bartender is
here, but so is that shrew whose husband
I represented in the divorce. Good God.

The sound of the bar dice is an anodyne.
Shots all around. All of us in this musty boat
must imagine Sisyphus happy. If not,
how could we cut the deal, how could we
bring 'em back, how could we avoid
the skunk?

This is New Year's Eve in Milwaukee,
for fuck's sake.

Sweating the Bottle

Every lawyer bears within him the debris of a poet.
                              —*Flaubert*

I love to push down the brown
paper bag to get to the mouth
of my forty and I love to screw
the cap back on after every swig.

It is the morning after a crackling
trial. I'm thinking about my gnome
of a client with his beady, black eyes
and salt-and-pepper beard—the kind
of beard that comes right up to the eyes
like a mask.

The morning dew has covered my car
windows like a gauzy cocoon.
A dog howls with the conviction
reserved for strangers.

While we waited for the verdict, my client told
me he had molested the boys for years.
He told me this because he knew
he was going to walk and it was time
to let me in on the joke.

I take the empty bottle and knead
the moist sides until the glass is warm
and the tiny droplets fall and pool
together and now I have enough
left for one more drink.

Basketball at 51

The elegy outlasts the battle.
     —Luis Borges

These young black guys are killing me.
I can't keep up. My Uncle Charlie won't
fall. No more Christmas facials.
I'm old enough to be Jesus's father
when he was crucified for God's sakes.
The thought of God existing is preposterous,
at least when I have lost faith in my left hand.

Where are the guys I used to play with?
Doing the elliptical instead or staying home
to stream Netflix? It's all I can do to hold
my man's jersey and he's getting pissed.
Nothing but net when I'm guarding him.
My heel hurts again—and I know the end
is near. One of these nights, I'll hobble off
the floor for the last time and slowly
make it to my car. I'll sit there while
the sweat cools. Turn on the radio and try
to find an old song.

Phone

I read on my phone there's a new TV channel just for dogs and that the weather is going be crummy for my son's prom tonight.

I read on my phone the court petition stating my teenaged client helped Smokey move the dead girl from the bathtub to the crawlspace and that the Brewers are losing to the Cards 3 to 1 in the fifth. I read that Apple sold 74.5 million of these things last quarter and that 62% of workers at the Fox-Conn factory in southern China work more than sixty hours/week making iPhones.

I read on my phone this quote from Beckett: "Habit substitutes the boredom of living for the suffering of being" and that we hit two homeruns to tie the game and that Apple made a profit of $13 billion last year and my son will be home from prom at about four this morning and the baseball is traveling farther because of global warming and that Smokey grabbed a kitchen knife and stabbed her once in her throat and then in her eye to finish her off and that my client took her earrings and bracelet and threw them in the trash and the iPhones are made with "conflict minerals" that come from areas engaged in warfare and Fox-Conn is proud to provide a swimming pool for its workers.

I read on my phone the average Fox-Conn worker makes £200/month and that £200 equals $411 and that at least a dozen workers have jumped to their death in the last three months and that *billet-doux* is French for love letter and that she might still have been breathing once they got her to the crawlspace and that the twelve people who killed themselves were between nineteen and twenty-four years old and that my son has his room assignment for his first year of college.

I read on my phone anti-suicide nets have been erected to cover 1.5 million square meters at the Fox-Conn factory and that my client is looking at ten years in prison and that we lost and that tomorrow's high will be 77 and the low 61 and that maybe it will rain but I won't know that until tomorrow.

The Chinese Proverb

There is a silver maple on my front lawn
that has a million leaves. I can rake
every weekend from late October until
after Thanksgiving and by Monday
my lawn is a golden carpet.

I call the tree *The Chinese Proverb*,
not because I can relate it to any specific
Chinese proverb but because all those
endless leaves evoke pith and pause
and a kind of pathos that a wiser man
could reduce to a keen turn of
phrase like *Talk does not cook rice* or
Do not keep handsome servants or
*Reading thousands of books is not as
useful as traveling thousands of miles.*
Of course, none of those proverbs relate
to my tree but you get the idea.

One could just say *Talking about something
doesn't get it done* or *Don't screw
the hired help* or *Experience is
more useful than theory* without the artful flourishes
but that would be like saying *You gotta rake
until there's nothing left to rake.*

This pedestrian phrasing would miss
the fall of the next leaf
the sun breaking through the clouds
the awesome futility of
pondering the insistent future.

Word

Interpretation is the revenge of the intellect upon art.
                              —*Susan Sontag*

I walk into a video store and ask the clerk
if they have *I'm Not There*. The clerk
checks his computer and says, "No,
but we have *I'm Not Scared*." His tone
is expectant and hopeful and it makes me feel
bad to tell him that while it sounds close,
it's not the movie I wanted.

Until a few years ago, I thought the term "fitful sleep"
meant a good night's sleep. Now that I know
the true meaning, I'm not sleeping so well.

I represent drug clients with the given first
names of *Kilo* and *Easy Money*, who sell
teenagers (one-eighth grams of heroin) to teenagers.
I have two teenagers.

HIDTA (pronounced *high-da*), an acronym
for *High Intensity Drug Trafficking Areas*,
is an anti-crime task force. My client keeps
complaining that Al Qaeda is after him.

When Kafka read *The Trial* to his friends
for the first time, he laughed so hard
that there were moments when he couldn't
read further. I, for one, do not think
the alienation of modern man is so funny.

Speaking in Tongues

*I smoked a blunt and drank too much bumpy
face so I called a johnny cab to take me to my baby
mama's crib. I saw a brother kickin' it. He said he
got a couchy-coupon from my lady. I said do you
know what time it is and he said it's time for some
drama so I took out my strap and busted a cap
on his ass.*

These words—in their doomed vibrancy—literally
mean: I smoked a marijuana and cocaine-laced cigar and
drank too much Seagram's Gin. I called an anonymous
phone number and told them where I was. A few minutes
later, a car picked me up and I gave the driver five dollars.
I told him to drive me to the house of my child's mother.
I saw a man on the corner who told me that my girlfriend
had propositioned him for sex. I challenged him to a duel
and he accepted. I pulled out my gun and I killed him.

Eventually, I will argue to the jury the following:
*My client had a drink with friends. He called a taxi
to take him home to his family. On the way home,
he encountered a long-time enemy of his who spoke
rudely about my client's girlfriend. The man pulled
a gun on my client. My client killed him in self-defense.*

Speaking in tongues, I translate a story of death.

Reasonable Doubt

Once when I was typing an email
my fingers were mispositioned one tab
to the left so when I typed *for* it read *die*.
It was a mistake, really. It could have
happened to anyone.

On my iPhone, my texts of the secret
ingredient read *vaginal* extract instead
of *vanilla* extract and yes it's my *Prius*
I'm selling on Craigslist not my *penis*.
Damn you, Auto Correct!

I like telling the jury that if you put
a cat and a mouse in a box and the mouse
disappears, the cat is guilty of murder.
Unless there is a hole in the box.

And that every word that snitch said
was a lie including *and* and *the*. Then
I quote Mark Twain who said, "A lie
can travel halfway around the world
before the truth puts its boots on" before
I implore the jury to put its boots on
and get to work.

And if the verdict comes back guilty, I tell
my client, you've got good issues to appeal
and the judge will temper justice
with mercy when he sentences
you. I won't forget you. I promise.

Burden of Proof

A crack-addict client kidnapped
a UWM student and drove her around
and held a gun to her head and raped her
and put her in the trunk of his car and
showed her to his friends and then let her
go at a gas station.

That's what she said.
He said

he picked her up at a bar
on Brady Street and she wanted to get high
so he bought crack with her money
and she was ready so he busted
his nut in the backseat and then
kicked her out of his car because
it was almost morning and he was
tired and she was getting to be
a clingy white bitch
which bugged the shit out of him.

I don't know what really happened
and I don't care. Or rather, I can't care.

It shouldn't make
a difference to me if he did it or not.
It shouldn't make a difference
that my son goes to UWM
and that girl could have been his friend.

Then I can tell you I represent evil.
And I can tell you that addiction makes
experience matter. And on we go.

The Breathing Lesson

The pock-marked Formica,
the gouged and graffitied table,
the walls the color of piss,
into the cell comes Nakia.

I catch my breath—not at the sight
of the gaunt young black woman
in her gleaming shackles and maroon jumpsuit—
but at her smell. It is a biting
stench of sweat and shit and urine.
A sirocco that fills the room
with a primordial odor of life and death.

Nakia tells me that while she was
in the back seat, the other girl
was in the front giving head to the john.
The drip of cocaine fell
from Nakia's nasal passage to the back
of her throat. She swallowed hard
and pulled the trigger.
One shot to the back of his skull.

Gary Gilmore told Mailer that
he wanted to die because of the noise.
Now, as I ask Nakia about her life,
we are drowning in electronic door slams,
shouted expletives, scraping footsteps,
and the white noise of transistor radios.

She draws me in with her history
of mother's beatings and
uncles' molestations and her abortion
at fourteen. I ask her something I never ask:
why did you do it?

She was killing to bring back her lost
children, clean her poisoned blood,
clear her drug-addled mind. She was
gasping for one last breath of air,
and now I will be her final accomplice.

St. Augustine

Everything is the oldest here—
the oldest house, the oldest mission,
the oldest park where they walk past
the bromeliads and seashell geegaws
for sale on the site of the oldest slave market
in North America.

There are firsts here too—
the first fort, the first Catholic
mass, the first permanent outpost
of European civilization, the first infliction
of the white man's burden.

The man and woman are getting older
and neither of them are firsts.

She swims in the waves in her peacock-
colored swimsuit; he tries to body surf
on a boogie board but ends up
looking for seashells.

At night, the terrace door is open.
The dreams come in increments.

For him, it's Martin Luther King and J.B. Stoner
and Woolworth's lunch counters and beaches
in this oldest and first and most segregated town.
Then the dreams go back even further,
to the first slaves, the Fountain of Youth,
the blood on the beach.

For her, it's the water and living things
under the water and how she wants to go
there and hide from this heavy, plain
history and fold herself forever
into the lullaby of the surf.

Court Appearances

Where is the poetry in this
boxy room with sallow walls and
carpeting the color of sludge?

Have any of you—Judge, DA, Bailiff—
ever read the darkly lyrical Larkin while
a client was being deposed or tried
to write a villanelle between appearances?

What if I told you to go
easy on the burglar because even
a flat screen HDTV doesn't have
the brilliant color of Sonnet #18
or the resolution of any poem
by Frederick Seidel?

Or that the only difference between
the serial arsonist and us is that
he cannot control the terrible freedom
of his thoughts. Isn't there beauty in fire?

The identity thief simply committed
the conceit of the probing author—
to be someone else in secret,
to create a doppelganger. The secret
sharer of Highsmith or Conrad or Twain.

If a line is a point set in motion,
then how could the forger stop
once he entered the decimal point?
It was an unbroken line to obfuscation
and abnegation, larceny and lucre.

Maybe the murderer should be set
free because we are all possibly dead
already. I will recite, Judge, to
the hereafter, and if no one comes,
let him go.

Home Visit

Oh, but it is buggy
in this upper flat.
The smell of grease,
grease permeating—
Stop cooking those burgers!

Grandmother is wearing a muumuu
of sorts. The holes for her arms
are the size of discuses and show black
muffs of armpit hair. Her grandson wanders
in bug-eyed and cracked up. He looks
at me askance. He looks askance.

Do they ever turn off the big screen TV?
There is a parakeet or a canary or some such
bird in a white-trimmed cage with a little
sandy-colored perch. She is mentally
filliping me. Flick, flick, flick.

Some photos line the wall. How long has
it been since anyone looked into the eyes
of the young newlyweds in their boffo pastels
and bright smiles? There is a sepia one, too,
of a grand couple in formalwear
taken before the diaspora north.

And a three-year-old girl here who is
my ward. Yes, I have wards who form
one of the precincts of my
gerrymandered mind.

She takes me by the hand and leads me
to her bedroom with her *Lion King*
bedspread and bare walls and silver
radiator blaring unreal warmth.

If not this family for her, who? Somebody
has to hang the pictures, somebody has to
pay the cable bill, somebody has to hear
the bird sing.

The Floating Man

Tonight I am all in a mist. I scarcely know what's what.
—John Keats

It started during a trial. I was sitting there listening to the DA's opening statement when I started floating about the courtroom,

over the judge, the jurors, the bailiffs, my client, the victim's family wearing matching shirts with his superimposed photo.

I could even see me—whispering to my client, taking notes, staring into space. I looked tired and I needed a haircut.

The next time I floated, I was at a baseball game with my two sons. They were still pretty little. I let them climb

to the top row of the upper deck. I drifted way up to keep an eye on them.

Far above the stadium, I could see the arc of the fly ball that fell to the glove of the outfielder with such regret,

I would have kept going if they hadn't pulled me back.

Between Witnesses

He wandered to the window
looked out on MacArthur Square

a man with a backpack sleeps
on a bench across from memories
of fountains and flowerbeds;

on the sidewalk figures move—

probably college students jogging
from the campus to the lake and back

Seagulls far off in the sallow sky
And he thought of the heavy lassitude
of life

Then the more nuanced
indolence commanded by the summer's day

And in a moment it was time to leave
his luxurious meander and return
to the next witness.

Ghazal for a Crow

The black crow at the side of the road picking over
the dead raccoon gives me a thrill and a shiver.

I want to arrogate happiness like a bird taking roadkill
from the scavenger, the parasite, the wanderer.

You are a taker, too, in the late boreal light.
Your tawny legs and hematite ring throw off my compass.

It frightens me that Pluto is no longer a planet.
Our stars are burning out on another Friday night.

And my son is gone. Gone. He left a memory stick
in his room. Nothing is heavier than a dusty guitar.

The lone crow barely flinches as I veer slightly.
The drops of blood coruscating before the shadow's touch.

III

The Summer Hour

There is a blue
berry patch near
Lake Superior

where every August
we go

to pick blue berries
in the loamy sand.

Miles from shore
a light breeze lifts
the water

until it becomes
a wave

bending toward this hour
in the twilight.

Berlin Sky

When daybreak surprised us that morning
in your hotel room, the Berlin sky was
the color of a healing bruise.

In my pocket were the chips of mortar I had
scratched out of the remnants of the Gestapo
headquarters. The mortar was turning
to sand by the hour—free at last
to disintegrate for all time.

I asked you to think of all the people
who had looked into that sky awaiting
the knock of the Gestapo or the Stasi,
the concussions of the Allied bombs,
or the signal to escape from East to West.

We were too drunk and happy, though,
to confront the city and its past—safely
distanced, as we were, from divorce
or the second thoughts of the newly married.

It was easy to look at the sky and write
our histories on the window pane
before passing into our Lethean sleep.

Memorial

They lay in bed looking at *The Book of Names*
sounding the words and jumbling the letters
of the unborn boy awaiting their touch.

Saigon, Tonkin, Phnom Penh. He touches
the map, picturing the obscure names
of the places described in his son's letters.

The black wall swells with inch-high letters
carved into the marble, begging to be touched.
The old man succumbs to the torrent of names.

Agnosto 2013

The deer antler spray must be working
because my Christ complex is on
the wane. My wonder is back. The Pope is
retiring and I wonder if he's still
infallible if he leaves the toilet seat up
in his new rooms in the convent.

If I were a Scientologist, I would be working
in Tom Cruise's garden and going clear.

The color of Beyonce's skin is beatific. I have
never seen anything so beautiful. There
needs to be a new crayon called "Beyonce"
so I can buy the 64-pack with the sharpener
and color all day long. I'll put on
Leonard Cohen and hold that crayon
like a crucifix.

When John Brown reached the scaffold
he said, "This is a beautiful country. I never
had the pleasure of seeing it before," as he
gazed over the valleys of Virginia. And
what of the wonderful vistas seen by the pilots
on the clear-as-crystal morning of 9/11? Or the
jumpers from the Towers?

And then the Tsarnaev brothers bomb the Boston Marathon.

If I believe again
I will blame it on you.

The Tree

Early one morning
an Amsterdam city worker
will drive his truck
to 263 Prinsengracht Street.
He'll take his chainsaw
and cut a wedge-shaped
piece of wood from the base
of the chestnut tree
that is now over
a hundred years old
and blighted (the tree may
creak in the wind).

He may not even notice
the attic window
where Anne Frank gazed
down on the tree.

He'll tie a rope around
the trunk and pull
it down. The whole operation
won't take more than
half an hour
not counting the wood chipping.

Milwaukee

We live without feeling the country beneath our feet.
                                                —Osip Mandelstam[1]

Just take Capitol west from the lake and you
will see it all. South on Teutonia past where
Borchert Field[2] used to be, west on Locust,
north on Groeling, grueling Groeling.
Blocks with two houses razed for every one
standing, the lots becoming fields, The Killing Fields
where an unregulated militia enjoys
its Second Amendment rights. The houses stripped
of copper, the bathtubs sledgehammered to pieces
for scrap. The cell phones glaring like torches in a cave,
the boys making their way

to the girl on the bed. There's a flipper[3]
in the crib and news travels fast.
Keep kidding yourself. Tonight before you go to sleep
in Brookfield or Whitefish Bay or Bay View
watch the local news with the goat-eyed newscasters[4]
showing us Scott Walker scouring pans at a local soup kitchen
in all his Wauwatosa whiteness. Did you know
the Packers have a playoff game coming up?
Did you know we live in the most segregated city
north of Johannesburg? Here is the Graveyard
of Industry, the rust and bone of the Midwest.
This is no town for the iophobic[5].

---

[1]Opening line from Osip Mandelstam's "Epigram Against Stalin." The poem has been called "sixteen lines of a death sentence." Mandelstam wrote the poem in 1934 and would recite it often. He knew that eventually the poem would be traced back to him and he would be arrested. He died in 1938 in a work camp in Vladivostok.

[2]Baseball park in Milwaukee for several professional baseball clubs from 1888 to 1952. County Stadium opened in 1953. Borchert Field (otherwise known as "The Orchard") was located at 3000 N. 8th St.

[3]"Flipper" is slang for a woman or girl who is, consensually or not, available for numerous successive sexual partners.

[4]Mike Jacobs, at least.

[5]*Def.* The fear of rust.

Old A.O. Smith is a favorite place to haunt.
Haul off and throw a rock through a window—
outfield to home plate. You could be Billy Bruton[6]
or Sixto Lezcano[7]. Ghosts only walk around
because they are trying to live again.
I love the sound of breaking
glass but there is nothing left
to break. Love lives
on propinquity but dies on contact.

Jeffrey Dahmer[8] is making chocolate at Ambrosia
(where he said the rats were as big as cats)
And Konerak[9] is on the horizon.

Two white teenagers are killed at Arby's
(even our crime is segregated) a stone's throw
from Miller Park where I watch my sons
run to the top row afraid that they would fall
and I have an impulse to run after them
but I trust the walls will not collapse.
But where is Alexis Patterson?[10]
Alexis, Alexis, Alexis.
A three-syllable curse.
Bound and silent under the snow
of her Snow-White youth.

---

[6]Centerfielder for the Milwaukee Braves (1953–1960).

[7]Right fielder for the Milwaukee Brewers (1974–1980). Won Gold Glove in 1979.

[8]Jeffrey Dahmer (1960–1994). Killed 17 men and boys between 1978 and 1991.

[9]Konerak Sinthasomphone. Killed by Dahmer on May 27, 1991, at age 14. When police arrived at Dahmer's apartment, he persuaded them that he and Konerak were lovers and Konerak had too much to drink. Konerak's head was eventually discovered in Dahmer's freezer.

[10]Seven-year-old girl who was reported missing on May 3, 2002 by her mother. Last seen at Hi-Mount School carrying a pink Barbie book bag.

One can't step into the same river
twice but I haven't even stepped in this one
once. The river, the god of ancient religions,
the mind's eye of many a rustic author,
the resting place of Fonzie's[11] statue,
I spit in you from the bridge that crosses
from Plankinton to Water and we are
both moving in the dark.

In the dark toward Red Arrow Park
where I used to take my kids ice
skating and where the ghost of Dontre
Hamilton[12] reaches out to the fathers
leading their little boys around the ice
rink and to the mothers holding
their hot chocolates. Open your hands
people, hold Dontre, let him in.

I take Lake Drive home.
It's the linearity that gets me.
The A to B to C of this life, of this city.
When I was a child I thought the water
of Lake Michigan was blue—
that if I had the chance I could hold
so many shades of blue
shimmering in my hands.

---

[11]Arthur Fonzarelli. A fictional character played by Henry Winkler in *Happy Days*. Fonzie was a mechanic and eventually became part-owner of Arnold's Restaurant (possibly after he jumped the shark). The "Bronze Fonz" statue was erected in 2008 and is located on the Riverwalk just south of Wells Street.

[12]Dontre Hamilton. A mentally ill homeless African American, shot 14 times by a Milwaukee police officer in Red Arrow Park in April, 2014. The officer was not charged with homicide any other crime.

When I get home, I will sit quietly,
no one will hear the scrape
of my pen or the sip of my drink or me
wrapping myself in a cool torpor for a moment
or two. Perhaps the drink will gentle
my unmerciful onslaughts. There is a world
within the world within the world.

I would love for you to read to me
just once—it could be anything,
Henry James[13] or Henry Miller.[14]
Afterwards, I would sleep dreaming
of big breweries and billowing smoke stacks
and the breathtaking field of steeples
I see from I-94 on my way to Chicago,
every nostalgic detail of the churches
ascending to the sublime.

---

[13]Henry James (1843 – 1916). American writer (known as "The Master") whose style has been compared to impressionist painting. He settled in England and became a British subject.

[14]Henry Miller (1891 – 1980). American writer known for breaking with existing literary forms. He developed a new sort of semi-autobiographical novel in his *The Rosy Crucifixion* trilogy.

I Had a Dream

I was in an airport. I saw a pretty young
woman in her early twenties. I knew
instinctively that she was a Danish actress. I
also knew instinctively that I was from Denmark
and an actor as well. We started chatting
and she told me her name was Addie Mae Collins
and we discovered, by coincidence, that we had
gone to the same small Midwestern liberal arts
college, years apart. I knew I had heard
her name before. Then I was in a library looking
her name up in old newspapers (it is a thrill to read
microfiche in a dream). I was right. She was
Addie Mae Collins, one of the four little girls
who died in the church bombing in Birmingham
in 1963.

I was back in the airport and I told her I knew who
she was. She smiled at me and whispered in my ear,
You will never know.

My Nausicaä

Nausicaä wasn't supposed to play
with the servant girls but she would
sneak to the river to find us while
we washed the clothes.

I chased the ball into the woods and
from a pile of leaves a man appeared—
naked and dirty, his hair full of brine.

We all ran and hid except for Nausicaä.
The sun on her raven hair, her silver
arm band, the ruby rings on her lily hands.
The man kneeled and asked if she was a goddess.
We took him to the river so he could bathe.
Nausicaä had us lay out a clean cloak and tunic
and a golden flask of olive oil.

When he was done, we were surprised
he looked so handsome and strong. Nausicaä
told him to go to the palace, enter
the megaron, and ask for her mother, the queen.

That night in the great hall, I filled
the cups with wine waiting for Nausicaä's
call. When the bard sang of Troy,
the man wept and revealed that he was
Odysseus. His tales of the war wrapped
the room around him.

The man kept glancing at the blushing
Nausicaä who caught my eye and smiled.
I trembled as I filled her cup. My hand
brushing hers—smelling the hyacinths in her hair.

I prayed to Athena
to hold back the horses under the ocean
so that dawn would not come,
or at least so that night could linger.

February 14, 2015

You're feeling a little more Lake-Superior blue
than a robin-egg hue.
The booth review said I was out of bounds
but I thought my apologies would redound

like a missed rebound to Giannis Antetokounmpo
or to the killing of the cartoonists at Charlie Hebdo;

instead you are the House Republicans and I am everyone else.
What did I do to make you so nonplussed?

It's not like I'm an ISIS beheader
a Russian-backed Ukrainian abettor
a subprime loan debtor
an Ebola-carrying jetter.

So let's keep our heads and sue for peace
pay our debts and sanitize the sheets.

Soon enough the roses will arrive and what will be said will be said
The champagne will pop and this poem will be read

and it will be here for all of a day
smiled over and then thrown away
with the flowers and the chocolates and a teddy bear from
Fifty Shades of Grey
after all, it's Valentine's Day.

Refugia

At night after our ritual
entwinement I move
from you decrementally.

My bedboat breaks away
and the currents carry
me past charnel beaches and
fallow fields

To the temple of Janus
to offer a husk of a poem,
you evaporating
from behind the ink.

In the morning, when
the warmth of your body
draws me back, I will begin
to remember your name.

Momentum

I.

On the Friday night we did not go
to San Francisco I went to a poetry
reading and you were in the hospital
because you weren't you.

You asked me to bring you
a present so I wrote you a poem
about not going to San Francisco
while you stayed in your room
and read *Anna Karenina*.

On Saturday night, I played cribbage
at the bar with the old-timers. You
made popcorn and tried to get
the other patients to dance.

On Sunday, you washed your hair
and waited for me to come so
we could talk.

II.

The mums—the ones you got
from your dad when you were
in the hospital in April—
are opening again.

It's too late, though.
The freeze is coming tonight
and by tomorrow their yellow lids
will permanently peek out

at the grass turning brown
the wilted stalks falling
the flitting of the sparrows.

The Flood

A baby's toy, a pair of tennis shoes, a photograph.
These things float by.

Near the washer and dryer, I can feel
the electric current moving
through the water—

Tables and chairs scattered in the backyard,
I am akimbo before a white sheet.
Photographs and school papers and notebooks
are drying in the late afternoon sun.
A damp and mottled picture of my wife
and me at a wedding—fifteen years ago.
We sit at a round table.
I glance sideways at the camera with
a half-smile. She is young and pretty
and looking at me.

I press the photograph between my hands
and push my breath into our faces.

In her school papers, I find
a folder of my old poems.
The ink has bled through the paper.
The words are illegible.

Two days later, she is in the basement
scrubbing the walls with ammonia.
The bite of the fumes catches up
with her. Tears well in her eyes
and she tries to hold them back.

Tears into a sleeve
a folded page in a book.

The Gyre

Under the wispy clouds
where the soft waves leave
momentary fault lines in the sand
I step in the water and push
the inner tube off the shore.

We lay on our stomachs, paddling
beyond the sandbar, our hands
making minute eddies vanishing
in the tide, the surface current
turning colder in the deep water.

When we are far from shore,
my son tells me last night he dreamed
that his mother was transformed
into a small action figure. She was
hurt or broken and he was holding her
and no one would help him.

We drift awhile in silence
and peer out at the expanse
of the deep blue sea.

It Began with Ice

The great basins of limestone, granite
and basalt gouged by the ice, filled
with meltwater. In retreat, the glacier
left its burden of rock, sand and clay—
a soaring moraine—beaten by the western
wind into this vast dune.

We climb to Devil's Slide, where one
hundred years ago the logs of virgin pine
rumbled into the surf of Lake Superior
bound for the sawmills to the east.

We rest on the cliff. You are next
to me, your naked feet in the sand.
Nine of every ten grains is quartz
and they shimmer through our fingers
like liquid silk. I watch you peer
into the blue horizon.

Four million years ago, the boulders began
their journey from the Arctic Circle. I would
have pushed them myself—to the beach
below—to see you smiling in the sun.

Become Stone

It starts with a journey to an island.
By June, the ice is melting and a new crop
of rocks has been left by entrusting
waves or exposed by abrading surf.
The best ones for the sculptor's blade
are marbleized fossils hard
and smooth as an arctic night.
A hunt yields one that will become
a mask

a memory
of the old shaman masks of fur,
ivory and sinew, made not to believe in
but to fear, masks that scared children
into knowing something could come
from the south or the east. Something hiding
behind smiling faces and crosses
or smelling of cooking oil and gasoline.
Masks worn, disintegrated, and forgotten.

In this land souls still abide in the arctic
fox, the tern, and the snow.
The little creatures in this bed
of fossils are coming back to life
as a mask of stone. A thousand
importunate spirits press in, trying
to get inside

where the atoms are spinning
as fast as on the day the urchins came to life
or as the night the stone sharpened the blade.

The River

The river where I'm digging is lined
with limestone that falls from the ledges
like so many plates.

There is the shelf that holds the fossils:
trilobites, brachiopods, cephalopods
and crinoids. I use a rock hammer
and a trowel. It's like finding a hit in
a stack of records or a favorite slide
from the carousel.

I wash the muck from the fossils as best
I can. Then I sit on the riverbank and look
at what I've found. It's late afternoon and trout
break the water, trying for the rising insects.

When I get home, I'll soak the fossils in
vinegar overnight. A few days later, I'll
put them on a shelf next to the driftwood
and agates and rock sculptures.

The remains of my life.

About the Author

Thomas J. Erickson grew up in Kohler, Wisconsin. He received a Bachelor of Arts in English Composition from Beloit College and a law degree from Marquette University. He is an attorney in Milwaukee, where he is a member of the Hartford Avenue Poets. His poems have appeared in numerous print and online publications, and his award-winning chapbook, *The Lawyer Who Died in the Courthouse Bathroom*, was published by Parallel Press (an imprint of the University of Wisconsin Libraries) in 2013. Erickson lives in Milwaukee with his wife, Daphne, and is the proud father of Charles and John.

www.ingramcontent.com/pod-product-compliance
Lightning Source LLC
Chambersburg PA
CBHW020959090426
42736CB00010B/1384